Cancer Makes the Sky Bluer

by
Patricia Heis

Edited by
Robin Stratton and Margot Brown

ISBN: 978-1-945917-10-3

Printed in the United States of America

Front Cover Photo: Rose Graham Miano
Back Cover Artwork: Patricia Heis
Cover Design: Tracey Capobianco Ranauro

BIG TABLE Publishing

"Making other books jealous since 2004."

Big Table Publishing Company
Boston, MA
www.bigtablepublishing.com

Tricia was a very social woman with lots of friends, local and all over the country via Facebook. She shared her journey of illness, pain, and the tragic late diagnosis of her cancer because she thought it might help others on a similar journey. But she refused to allow herself to be defined by her cancer. Despite all the surgeries and the chemo that made her beautiful hair fall out, she found joy everywhere. Even at the end, her life was about living, not dying.

In addition to Tricia's Facebook posts, she kept a journal that she had hoped would one day be a book. After her death, her mother Rose gave the notes to Margot Brown, who created a document, which she emailed to me so that Tricia's dream of being published would come true. These journal entries, mostly undated, have titles. I supplemented them with relevant posts on Facebook, some of which were edited for typos or presented in excerpts.

So here is your book, Tricia. You continue to inspire us. We love you forever.

Robin Stratton, December 2016
Boston, MA

For Casey

September 1, 2014

This is not a fun Facebook status update. But, along with the tumor they said I have cancer. Everything has to be removed! Rectum, uterus, ovaries, vagina all have to be built. I better start reminding myself this is just a shell and you can always find a nice view.

You Have Cancer!

You have Cancer. Three words that terrify and leave you speechless and in shock for a while. But I had waited a long time for a diagnosis. I knew something was wrong almost ten years ago.

"Bleeding hemorrhoids," the doctor had said. It sounded reasonable, since I was doing the P90X—a workout I loved and pushed myself to complete. I loved that it was something my then-husband Jim and I did together, and then compared results. We'd sunbathe on our deck, and he'd admire my hard body. I was most proud of my abs, and he appreciated my hard work to lose those twenty pounds and get in better shape.

Better shape? How the heck was I growing a Cancerous tumor and not even know it? What if I'd had a CAT scan then instead of an ultrasound? A CAT scan would have shown why I was having pelvic pain.

I had a standing computer desk, and would stand for hours working on my social networks and website: Selling the Law of Attraction. I fell in love with it in 2007 right before *The Secret* came out. Madonna was teaching Kabbalah so I learned some from her, and was hooked when I heard on a radio station that *What you focus on expands.* I can create anything I want... or don't want if I'm not careful. Jim and I studied and practiced it together and miracles happened. Small and large.

But why would I create Cancer? I asked myself over and over. My beautiful girlfriend on Facebook, "Unasleip," explained it to me: "You wanted to be an inspiration; to love and help others be loved, and to make a difference."

Be careful what you ask for. Cancer became a gift in that way. The other kind of gifts came daily in the form of presents, cash or messages of love from my social network of friends—strangers who touched my heart and soul.

My story may make you see how lucky you are. You have your health and, as the saying goes, "If you have your health, you have everything."

It's very true... or at least it's a great start.

My purpose in sharing my story is to convey this message: you are not alone, whatever your struggles. But, you have to allow it in, sometimes you have to ask for it. One day, in the chemo waiting room, I talked with a man complaining about waiting for his chemo, waiting for his doctor, complaining about how his kids, who live far away don't care—that they are just waiting for their inheritance. He had esophageal Cancer and could not eat without a tube. When he complained about that, it was truly justified. *How lucky I am*, I thought, *I can eat again!*

Living with Cancer, Living with Love

♥

This is the life! I'm lying next to my husband in our California king size, freshly bleached and sheeted bed, with a smallish medium size black dog named Zeus, who is half under the covers like the little human he thinks he is. My beautiful Labradoodle, Zoey, the love of my life, lies at the foot of the bed on a hide-a-bed couch, sleeping peacefully.

We purchased the hide-a-bed couch to keep from having to rent another hospital bed for me.

This is the life because what could be better? I'm watching a movie on the 55" TV at the end of the room, the comedy, *Bridesmaids*. Some parts are very funny. Next to me is a cookie, a glass of water, and a stack of books to read. Most of the books are about the C word: Cancer, the word no one wants to hear.

Explanation

I am not a writer. I am a woman, a mother, a daughter, a friend, a student of life, and I believe we all have a story to share. Every decade of my 54 years has been a new story. I have lived a hard but happy life in all of those years. But this story may have been the hardest, saddest, most fearful, and the most loving of them all.

Growth

That describes it perfectly. Growth of a tumor that took my colon—and attempts to take my life—but none, more importantly, than Spiritual growth.

I am so grateful to have a life. I feel good today; good as I can as long as I don't think about all the pains from my last surgery that I am still recovering from. I am so lucky to be alive that everything is wonderful.

I worked hard to get to this day. I don't know how long this will last—the feeling good, almost normal. How do you live with Cancer? The best I can say is you do it with love. "Love is real; everything else is an illusion." I heard that once from my favorite crazy-ish guru, David Ickle. Nothing matters but love. That I know for sure. It's not that I love Cancer. It's that I love life, everything in it, and that I've made peace with the Cancer. How do you do that?

"I will let you be if you let me live. Don't spread or grow or attack other parts, what parts I have left. Live and let live."

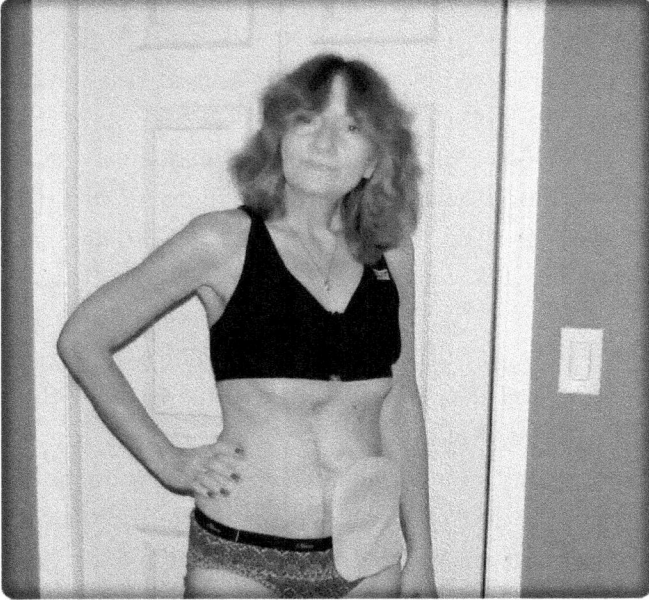

How do you like my new bag?

August 5, 2015

I'm just lying here listening to my heart beat and it sounds so strong and I know I am so loved. But how do we know when it's time to let go? On August 28th of last year, I went into the emergency room to get a blood transfusion after being in terrible pain for two years and treating what I was told was a C diff infection with a $5000 antibiotic. The tumor busted through and I was rushed to have a CAT scan. A while later a doctor walked in to say, "You have cancer." I said, "No, I have C diff." The sad look on his face said otherwise, and that I tested positive for both. A doctor just a few months earlier while looking at my blood work said, "Well, you don't have cancer," so that was the last thing I thought was wrong. I had also been told I had bleeding hemorrhoids, which was another mistake—it turned out to be a growing tumor. This last year is now a blur of unbelievable pain, surgery, tests, chemo, radiation, drainage, fistulas, and colostomy bags, only to still be standing in that same place of fear and uncertainty. At what point do I get peace?

When is the fight over? I love everyone too much to want to leave them but maybe after all this time on the rollercoaster from hell, peace is what they need too. The ride hasn't been all bad. I have learned so much about compassion, grew closer to my friends and family, learned to love the strangers that have my life in their hands, and mostly was taught how precious life is and how every moment counts. So for now I will keep listening to that heart beat because it is too filled with love to let it stop.

My new IV port for chemo

August 20, 2015

2 to 5 years, I'll take it. Would you ask? I finally got the nerve to ask my cancer doctor yesterday and that is the average life span for my situation if nothing can be done. But I'm sure we will find something, stats don't really matter, and I'm definitely not average.

August, 2015

I Call it "Bull"

"You may only have a few years to live, so let's run scans every few months."

This means nothing to eat, which means dropping five more pounds and having to force yourself to eat again once you're allowed, or nothing to drink except that horrible stuff they use for the scans.

So I watch these meaningless TV shows and movies. I struggle sometimes to find programming that *I* want; programming to fight Cancer *my* way, rather than always doing it the doctors' ways.

Oprah's *Super Soul Sunday.* One of the best! I enjoy authors who want to help us live better lives. I admit I do have a few shows that may not be great for the brain, but the entertainment value I find sometimes worth it. Since the 70s, Mary, beautiful Mary, and I have been watching our soap, *General Hospital.* I want to live another 50 years so I can watch the characters grow, marry, commit adultery, save the world, destroy the world, some have babies, some die, and very often come back to life. Mary and I are connected through our soap so, for that reason alone, it's a great hour out of my day, out of my life. Other current TV shows I love are *Limitless* (pure genius), and *Second Chance.* I have watched the Oregon TV show *AM Northwest* all the way back to The Boz. After The Boz and Margy left, I felt completely compelled to hear Helen and her guests wishing each other the best. I remember going through chemo "together" with Dave Anderson, and he would joke about wearing the pump, something I found sadly amusing, as well: "Chemo-to-go." I would place my order with a nurse at the infusion center.

After Dave finished chemo, he seemed fine. Then he disappeared. When at last he reappeared, he announced that he was going back on chemo. This is the same time I believe I had my last-first new chemo. When I made my decision to end all treatments.

And then he was gone.

I watched every day that I could and followed Facebook. Where was Dave? And Helen wasn't talking. Then, one sad morning they said Dave passed away the night before. How could this be true? He was okay! We were going to be okay together! Even though he was a celebrity that I did not know in person, going through Cancer together, we would have been friends.

I wondered, *What did Dave do that I didn't do?* He had a wonderful family and friends who loved and adored him.

What made me so special? That came up the first time when Stephanie's grandmother passed away from Cancer just a few weeks after the family found out she was sick. The only difference I could find between Dave and myself, besides having totally different Cancers, is I quit chemo as he went on to have his second round. I may never know why I lasted longer than some, but I miss you both, Stephanie's grandma and Dave Anderson.

How Do I Keep Going on Days Like This?

I used to love hot showers and baths. I took a bath every night for years, to get a slight relief from the terrible, constant, cramping pain. It's different now, though there will never be a relaxing bath again with the new body to look at. I dread showers, sometimes standing that long is impossible. The gentle stream of water stings my forearms—I suppose because my skin has gotten so thin. Today, I noticed while showering that the bulge around the stoma (part of the ostomy attached to my skin) is larger. I never shower with the bag on because it is the time it is safe to have it off. For some reason the constant output kindly stops for me when I get in the water. The rest of the time it seems constant and the bag needs to be emptied several times a day.

My body looks like a bad dream to me. How can all this be real? Thankfully, this week, I had my power port (implanted device for IV treatments) removed, and the soreness is going away. I appreciated it, as it saved me from many pokes, but sometimes, added more. I don't like being dependent on colostomy products or devices like a cord that connects to my heart to allow chemo and fluids to be exchanged with additional needles. The port sometimes was painful on its own. Every month it had to be flushed at the infusion center. I could never be truly done if I kept it.

One of the nurses recommended I keep it so it would be easier for hospice if they needed to step in. That she mentioned it was another reason I knew keeping it would mean staying part of this medical community that I believed would keep me sick. My last chemo nurse truly convinced me of that when she kept telling me about all the bad side effects. No other nurse had talked to me that way, and her knowing it all left me so afraid I felt the effects even before leaving the building that day.

I spent the next four days on the couch, exhausted and cramping. My face broke out in painful small acne type spots, and my hair actually hurt. I knew I would lose my hair all over again, this time from the new chemo drug, not from malnutrition. I knew my face would be so broken out that I wouldn't want to leave the house, even if I could get off the couch.

And it felt like there was no end to this.

Of course, I would do anything to save my own life if I knew I could, but we would see how I was after six months, and then, as maintenance, I could have to continue chemo forever. This would be no life. I would be more of a burden to my family and I couldn't bear it.

So, I quit chemo and am taking my life in my own hands—relying on relaxation and special teas, guavita, dandelion and turmeric, all known to destroy Cancer cells.

August 29, 2014

The naturopath called to say my blood work came back and they have never seen numbers so low. I was a 6, and 12 is normal.

"Get to the hospital and get a blood transfusion," he advised, "before you have a heart attack or a stroke."

Too sick and weak to keep justifying not going because I don't have health insurance, I gave in.

September 5, 2015

It was worth the discomfort of leaving the house to go to Safeway yesterday to have this conversation. The checker and a shopper were talking about their birthdays. The checker was turning 52 today and the other guy was turning that soon. They spoke of how awful it is to be getting older so I could not resist butting in to say how lucky they were because I did not know if I would be able to have another birthday. The checker's tone changed as he told me how he just came from an old friend's funeral. He was just walking down the road, fell, hit his head and died. Just like that. I said well that is a good reminder for me that being diagnosed with something does not necessarily mean that is what will take me away from this life. Like Wayne Dyer showed us last week when they found no further trace of cancer in his body. The checker and I talked more for a while about the importance of birthdays and how he was going to celebrate. Then he said, "Thank you for giving him someone else to pray for," and asked if he could give me a hug. I was very touched by our moment and it made going out no matter how difficult, totally worth it. You sure won't hear me complain about any more birthdays. Every birthday and every day is a blessing and a reason to celebrate life.

September 22, 2015

We spent the afternoon at the Health and Healing center at the bottom of the hill next to the tram and I wished I had more news for you about what I'm going to do. The good news was the surgeon is willing to try the operation to remove the tumor that is now firmly attached to my tailbone. I actually know how attached it is because with two different doctors yanking on it I'm now bleeding a lot. The surgeon said the risk is high that I bleed to death while they try to remove it but he believes it is my only hope to survive more than two years and it will be a brutal death because they can't do much for pain control in that area. I guess I chose one of the most painful tumor locations possible. He thinks they only have to take half of my vagina, like that's a good thing, and a few other parts but he insists on having an MRI done on the liver. They don't believe me that it is fine. Kent took this as good news because at least they are willing to try, but I left there feeling beat up not ever wanting to go back. Now I don't know what to do. I really did not like the surgeon's bedside manner, he was harsh, rough, and cocky which I have found is a trait in most of the surgeons I've met this last year. Perhaps they are that way because they hold your life in their hands and they are often your last hope. I also do not like university hospitals because as a patient you are a guinea pig that they use to teach students. Bad memories of that came back when my son was a baby and a patient at Shriners. Kent does agree I should go talk to my cancer doctor about this and see what the maintenance chemo involves, but all that does is buy you some time. Unfortunately, this major surgery may only do the same. The surgeon said there is no guarantee: I could go through all this and the tumor might grow right back. I'm so afraid and just wish this could all go away. The will to live is strong but after a year of this I'm so tired and just want to be left alone. Anyway, I wanted to update you and now I have to try to figure out what to do. Thanks for listening. ♥

September 25, 2015

After talking to my cancer doctor and family about what to do, it sounds like my best hope for survival is to proceed with surgery. I still believe there are many cures for disease that works as long as you believe in them but without complete faith it's a road I may not want to go on without the doctor's help. The next step is getting the MRI on the liver and if it's clean then I start meeting with the five surgical teams that are going to be trying to save my life. I'm having to surrender and do everything their way meaning for now giving up my hospital and team here that has been my support system for the past year. Even the MRI can't be done here after the doctor changed his mind. He wants full control and I have to accept that not everyone is kind and gentle the way they have been here for me. Thank you for all your suggestions and support. You have been my rocks that I can continue to take on this journey. Luv you! ♥

October 3, 2015

This is my big news... The planned date for surgery to remove the tumor and a few other parts is set for November 4th if all goes well. This special machine called the Mobetron has only been out for about a year and zaps its magic dust on the tumor while it is being removed to give me a better chance at a longer life. As long as insurance approves it then they want to use it on me. Of course I am scared out of mind to have the surgery but more afraid not to so I'm taking this opportunity with an open mind and an open heart that is there because of all of you that shared your positive thoughts and kept me going. I have one month to prepare the house, have a garage sale, and get myself as strong and healthy as I can be and maybe then this journey can come to an end and my new life can begin.

I have to share this again and explain. I quit chemo today and my doctor had me feeling quite guilty about it. I was doubting my decision when she used words of potential cures that she didn't before. This time she said there is a chance this chemo with the radiation could cure it, potentially. Where before she said it wasn't safe to have the chemo and radiation together. I have only four weeks to make sure I want to quit and then there is only life-long chemo to stay alive. I'm going to have a scan and talk to my other doctor but I felt better about my decision when I got on here and the first thing I saw was someone posting how they were glad they listened to their heart and never did chemo with their cancer. They were alive and well many years later. It gave me back some peace. I had read this post about putting my hand on my heart just before my mystic friend Leslie said, "You are already a miracle. Now, you just let your body catch up to what your heart already knows." It was my HEART that led me to choose this and I will trust it and all the signs confirming this. My heart also says thank you for reading my long posts and for your support and prayers... And that better days are on the way for all of us!

With Santa

January 28, 2016

I am in shock after receiving my first chemo bill that I just opened. This confirms I won't be doing it again. The cost for one day of the medicines, a visit with the doctor and blood work needed to show you can keep getting it is $10,300.00! That is per day. Once a week for six months to indefinitely. That is not counting scans or treatments to help counteract the bad side effects caused by the chemo. My doctor never even mentioned the cost of this before starting and insurance barely wants to pay half. So it would cost us $5000 a week, plus. Insurance just went up to almost $300 a week! There is so much wrong with the whole health care system!

Goodbyes

March 1, 2016

A new month of beginnings and a month of ending. Bittersweet goodbyes were made today to the nurses who, with tender loving care, administered the drugs that were to keep me alive. With compassion and kindness, these ladies became my Angels. They offered me warm blankets, cool drinks, information and conversation. Susan wasn't there this day, and that may have made it easier. The front desk ladies said goodbye, and one gave me the most wonderful hug. She is a truly caring woman in whom I confided about my decision to discontinue all treatments.

She understood and said she would hold me in her prayers.

And there was Ann, the social worker who I knew would fight for me if money was the only reason I couldn't get the chemo. But it was too late for help, the choice had been made, and this time it had been mine. No more dangerous drugs, no needles, no doctors, no more being weighed, blood pressure, heart rate, temperature, blood work.

I feel strangely peaceful alone with family and friends.

The way life should be.

Anyway, Back to the Shower and the Reason for These Words: How Do I Go On?

I am having new pains in my hip, pelvis and legs. My ostomy cramps a lot and I live in fear that the hernia will cause another blockage. I can't live through another one of those. It can also cause twisting of the intestines, requiring emergency surgery. How can I ever leave town knowing I could be too far from the hospital for emergency surgery? I'm trying to learn what I can do to help it. I read something about a hernia belt. There it is: another device to have to deal with. I will never live in peace if fear is my every breath.

The other thing I noticed in the shower today is that my rectal flap that was created out of my stomach muscles is swelling up like a balloon. The plastic surgeon said that could happen, and sometimes liposuction will correct it. I do not want to go back to Portland. It is hard on my husband to take the time off work to get me there. They are expensive visits, and like I said, "I need to be done!" I guess I'll see if I can live with it. Being afraid of its growth, I asked my husband to please take a look at it, and he refused—scrunching his face like I was showing him the grossest thing. Maybe it is, but I needed his help. For such a strong man, a man I have never seen cry, 6' 3", 250 pounds... able to reach things and lift really heavy things... he impresses me with his skills and his strength until this came up.

My husband can't bear to look at my body. It made me cry today and I asked myself, *How can we have a marriage if my own husband can't look at me?* As new newlyweds, we never really had a honeymoon. Being in constant pain makes everything a challenge but I looked forward to the time I wouldn't need birth control and we could go at it like rabbits. That time will never come. Not only is my husband not attracted to me (this scarred-up, deformed looking body is starting to gain some muscle back, and with clothes on, I look pretty normal) but the surgery, taking some of my girl parts along with everything else, shortened my vagina. My last examination left me with bloody panties all day, so I knew getting intimate with my husband was not going to happen anytime soon (no pun intended.) So, a sexless marriage with extra health challenges does not leave us with good odds of a long and happy marriage. It all seems cruel sometimes that even this was taken away from me. I read that having orgasms could help my recovery from this surgery. Where do I find pleasure? Sex, food (some days I can't eat)? There is still love, nature, family and friends.

Guavita, Dandelion and Turmeric

I kind of skipped around here, but wanted to say things about the tea I am drinking. It doesn't cost $10,000 a week like the chemo, and it makes me feel better, not worse. So why not? The surgeon says some chemo is better than nothing, but he doesn't know the tea company's everyday claims that they do get rid of Cancer. I thought, *They can't make these claims if it's not true.* I do not know my outcome, and I don't know if I can live with this new body. I'm lucky—that last surgery could have taken my bladder and I would have ended up with stents that would have to be replaced every three months. Or I could have a permanent bladder bag that I would have to learn to change on my own. I can't bear another thing like that to keep me alive. I am finally down to one device, the colostomy, and have to try to keep it that way.

So I leak and have no feelings of having to go, and would bet I have a constant infection.

With Kent in August, 2013

Perhaps the thing I miss most with my hubby is cuddling. He is a big teddy bear and no child, dog or woman can resist wanting to crawl up on his lap. Now that it hurts to be touched I think he is afraid to cuddle. My only tolerable position is to lie sideways, which doesn't help to be closer. I do miss his strong arms around me, which is where I felt the safest ever. Learning to sit and watch my laundry sit for a day or two before putting something else on. Being a neat freak before Cancer that would never happen. Zoey needs a bath and I can't wash her. That is heart breaking.

How do we learn to let go when we can no longer do things because of health issues? By not ignoring these tasks, I caused a potential life-threatening hernia around my ostomy. Don't lift for three months, including the laundry basket. These are still things worth living for, but for today, how do I go on?

Did I ever love my body enough to take care of it? When I was a kid in the 60s, my mother prepared healthy meals for the family until what seemed her inevitable divorce. She became a working mom with no time or money for shopping. I remember having mayonnaise and mustard sandwiches. Once she remarried, life became more about trying to survive abuse and neglect. Taking care of myself became less important as a teenager than just trying to stay away from the house. My body then became abused by men, drugs and alcohol.

I had quit smoking a year before getting pregnant at thirty years old. My first husband and mother quit with me, but I was the only one around for me at that time, and never went back to those bad habits.

Getting pregnant by my boyfriend while living in Newport changed how I looked at my body for several years. And trying my hardest to have a healthy child was all that mattered. After Casey was born I went into shock from an inverted uterus. The doctor said to push, and I don't know if I pushed too hard or he pulled too hard, but when I was sent off by ambulance to a bigger hospital, my baby was left in the nursery. Thankfully he had a grandmother who adored him with all of her heart, but he didn't get to come to me for several days.

Casey's birth and the resulting trauma was my first touch with death. I was given my Last Rites but couldn't make that transition. What would be sadder than a new mother dying while giving birth?

For years, my life completely revolved around trying to take care of this precious child. His father was in and out of his life, preferring a life of drugs to being part of a real family. I don't blame him. He also had a rough childhood and I don't think he ever really learned how to love.

I know for sure I won't be leaving this life with any hatred or regret. My step-father wasn't emotionally healthy. He beat my mother and that was worse than anything he could do to me because I was already helpless. How dare any man abuse a woman, child or animal? How messed up must we be, are we, to hurt the ones we love?

Anyway, my young son had so many problems that broke my heart and my mother's (she finally got away from her abuser and found a very sweet man who loved her and me very much.) He was born with a club foot and would spend years having surgeries and wearing casts. He never learned to crawl, but was bright and beautiful. I knew life would see him through.

While we lived in Reno (where my mother and her boyfriend also lived), two-year old Casey started having grand mal seizures, and had to be medicated to keep them under control. Nothing is more heartbreaking than watching your sweet baby turn blue, stop breathing, and have violent convulsions. Once he started school, his seizures stopped, but then came new problems: Tourette Syndrome and Asperger Syndrome, both presenting as high functioning forms of autism. My second husband helped me to home school Casey after watching him struggle in school. We knew it was too hard for Casey socially, and the tics from Tourette's progressed.

Then, with Casey's needs understood and attended, for the first time in my life, I really did take good care of myself. Knowing my son was taken care of I could focus more on myself. I started to watch what I ate, and completed the P90 workout; hard, but rewarding. I was proud of my abs and my body for the first time in my life. I didn't know that hiding beneath what appeared to be a healthy body was a silent killer; a small tumor beginning to grow. My oncologist said I probably had it for about ten years, putting the tumor's onset in my early 40s. How could I have felt so good? How many of us have time bombs like Cancerous tumors hiding beneath our healthy appearances?

I asked myself what I did wrong. I'm sure every Cancer patient asks themselves that question. Did I drink too much in the 80s? Did I ever eat enough fruit and vegetables? Was it the chemicals in our air, our drinking water? Did I sit too long at the computer when we created our online business? According to media reports, red meat causes colon cancer. I did not eat meat. I had not had a hamburger since the 80s. I stopped eating all meat because I love animals. I still feel everyone who chooses to eat meat should first spend some time at a slaughterhouse; make an informed decision for the sake of the animals who are tortured to death. I did, occasionally, add fish to my diet.

Weighing 99 pounds while in the hospital, I know my non-meat eating days may come to an end. Protein was what would heal me from the surgery, according to my surgeon, and my current husband who always wanted to cook for me. Thinking what could make me better, I gave in with an occasional chicken breast, but pork and cow will never be part of my diet. We don't know if foods really play a role in getting Cancer. As a vegetarian, there was no reason for me to get colon rectal cancer if that was true. Today, I just live by doing everything in moderation, and I listen more to what my body wants. Some days, I crave strawberries.

I'm not going to sugarcoat my story or tell you how Cancer changed me for the better. My intent in putting my story on paper is to help others, for whom I hope my journey is never repeated. And for those who have been through it and understand how brutal Cancer can be, I want to tell you that you aren't alone. For those who are diagnosed in the future, I intend for those numbers to be much lower than doctors predict now. It is unacceptable that one out of every two people will be diagnosed with Cancer. No one should ever have to go through it or watch someone they love endure it. To those that didn't survive—or won't survive—I don't think they did anything wrong. The will to live is so strong that we humans will do whatever we can to stay alive— until we can't, anymore. There is no such thing as not fighting enough. We do as much as we can take and then letting go is actually another step along the way of doing as much as we can.

I would never say "Give up," but I do believe there may be a time to let go. The most empowering thought I have at this point is knowing that pills should be available for me when the time comes. I so admire the California mom and her married daughter who both moved to Oregon so the daughter could get the pill that would end the misery of her trying to live with her brain tumor. ("A glitch in the system" is what I call her brain tumor, and it can happen to anybody.) I have talked to a woman younger than myself who, as I did, lived a healthy life, yet all we hear about is how eating well, at least five fruits and vegetables a day, not smoking, not drinking, not eating red meat, and regular exercise, should be enough to keep you healthy—unless it's NOT!

Whatever the reason, something needs to stop this. I don't remember hearing about so many succumbing to Cancer when I was young. I believe I had a great grandfather who died of lung cancer, but it sure didn't seem like one out of every two people got it.

I don't support animal research. It breaks my heart to think of any living creature being tortured. I also think we are different than animals and our crazy environment may be the cause of most Cancers.

Doctors found no genetic reason for my Cancer, but I have a few thoughts of my own besides chem-traits, bad water, too much stress, etc. I slept on an electric heating pad on my bed for most of my life. I've always been cold and can't bear to crawl into a cold bed on winter nights. Could the electricity (electromagnetic radiation) have been absorbed into my body, causing this glitch? What about me sitting in front of a computer all those years? Some studies suggest that people who sit a lot seem more vulnerable to colorectal cancer. What else? Hours in a hot tub? Wiping with scented wipes? The list goes on and on, and still frequently haunts my thoughts.

My father

People I Fell in Love With

About six months into my first treatment I did start to see everything differently. It may be the body's way of saying *Things are great, keep going!* Does it come from the subconscious to teach us how to love? I only know when it happens you feel it with all your body and soul. It is an awakening—a shift in consciousness. It seriously changes you, but only after so much more pain, torture and dis-appointment. I haven't been able to hang onto it. But I still get glimpses. My astounding Facebook friends will say something and I become overwhelmed with love for them.

Cancer makes the sky bluer. Colors became more vivid, sounds, tastes (so terribly altered by chemo) immeasurably enhanced. So much more beauty— everywhere. We live on such an amazing and glorious planet. The rain forests, the U.S. National Parks, the coral reefs, etc. So much beauty and reasons to be amazed! It blows my mind still, how honored we are to be sharing this wonderful planet with all of the incredible life forms inhabiting it.

I fell in love with Life.

I fell in love with friends, family and complete strangers.

My parents became so important to me. How dare I die before them and leave them the unbearable burden of losing their only child? I have the most amazing parents! Not the best choices were made by them regarding my life, but when I asked if my mom would mind moving in with Kent and me to help me get through more surgeries, she did not hesitate.

Mom loved her living conditions for the first time in her life. She was independent and could live without a man. She had her own apartment and managed everything on her own. At one point, we did move my twenty-one year old son in with her, and he became a great help. But overall, I was proud that she finally did it. I believe she thought she could not live without a man, and she was finally doing it by choice and was happy. She gave up her friends in her apartment community, which I know was very hard for her because she is very social. She has helped me get through so much. I would not be here today without her love and support.

My father, at 85 years old, lives far away in his cabin in the woods. All along I had planned on moving in with him to help him with the little things. He shouldn't be doing some things on his own anymore, like driving to town. I am sure poor Dad scares everyone off the road!

Add to that, Casey's seizures. Mom's boyfriend Richard saved my sanity by telling me over and over, "He will grow out of these." Richard was like a brother to me, and Casey's constant mentor (since Casey had no father in his life.) Richard's strength helped us through many hard times, and still calls with words of wisdom. That helps me make it through the day. Casey's father has been another surprising source of support for me, calling to check on me and telling me what I need to hear: how to get through a procedure, or ways to feel better. I so appreciate his kind heart and great advice.

I have talked about my Dad moving in with us; selling the house that he and his father built with money he earned from the sale of an airplane mechanic shop he owned years ago. I was always so proud of my Dad. He could fly planes. He spent months in the New Guinea jungles with the head hunters working on engines. He could prepare us the best pizza and milkshakes on weekends when I was young enough still to spend time with a dad. He married a sweet woman with two daughters and as they moved in together, in their new home, I knew weekends with Dad were over.

Being a healthy, partying teenager, I didn't let myself adapt to his new life, and was sent back home, where I wasn't safe. I wish now I would have given my stepmother, Nancy, a fair chance. She loved plants and I know she could have taught me so much about them. That was over 40 years ago, and I will always miss what could have been. It wasn't fair that no one was given enough time with her. She died of Cancer on New Year's Eve. I lost contact with her two beautiful daughters until a few years ago. I know them on Facebook, and Kim has been a real sister to me since. The love and support she shares with me is unimaginable. If knowing her could have rubbed off some of her goodness on me, I would have been the luckiest sister alive.

Luckily, for me, I was given a sister with my mother's second marriage. "Angel Amy," and I do mean Angel. She is so compassionate. I just want to say *Thank you* to her. She would do anything for those she loves. As an older step sister, I didn't do a good job at being a role model, but this little girl hung tough and went along with my bad ideas of taking her to parties with me. I only got to see her in the summer as we grew up, but she was never a burden to me; never a burden. The only thing that ever made me mad about her was when it was suggested I give her my talking Mrs. Beasley doll, since I was told I was getting too old to play with dolls. I would have given her all my dolls if it meant I got to grow up with that wonderful little spark of joy. She always had a big smile and she was a gift. She is the same little Angel today as a grown woman with a heart of gold.

How lucky we are to have people like this in our lives. Appreciate whoever gives you love and comfort. And to every Amy out there, thank you! Amy has brought soup and sent get well gifts. The most wonderful thing she did was to come to my last surgery. There is always the chance of not waking up, especially since many parts were going to be removed and rebuilt and there was no guarantee all of the Cancer was going to be removed. There was a possibility it had moved into my bone, and the nightmare of that has just begun. But Amy was there with my mom and my husband. I got to say I loved her before going in.

Another beautiful Angel showed up and stayed through the intense nine-hour surgery. Kent's second to oldest daughter, Stephanie. What a gift this girl is. She has given Kent three amazing kiddos; Lily, Garrett and Kirsten. I hope they think of me as another grandma. The most thoughtful gift was receiving "Hope," a stuffed bear with hearts of love. Hope made the perfect partner for Teddy. A gift from Kent, Teddy has had many traveling adventures with me. Hope was the bear that got to go on a healing adventure with me. Little Kirsten gave me Hope. With six weeks of daily radiation, the first day I was saddened by the hard rubber device to hold on to, which meant "Keep your hands still." Along with Hope, Stephanie spent the day of my surgery with her dad, making sure he would be okay and not alone. She helped move my mom in with us, driving her car for the three-hour trip.

But the sweetest thing was when I woke up for a moment in my hospital room and saw her sitting quietly in a chair next to the bed. I was so touched that she was spending time with me. I was in and out of consciousness, so I am sure I did not make much conversation, but she didn't mind. She just sat with me. It still brings tears to my eyes. I wasn't alone, ever alone, when I thought I was.

Stephanie also showed a nurse how to prop me with pillows so I could get off my very sore bottom. Stephanie had worked in health care and had skills my own nurses didn't have. What a gift that girl is. Sadly, she just recently lost her grandma, to whom she was so close, to Cancer. I hope it ends there in their family.

The fear of Cancer being genetic is terrifying. My son Casey has higher odds of getting colorectal cancer, they say, and how do you get a young man to have a colonoscopy? I can't even get my 55-year old husband to get checked. But my son is wise beyond his years, so I'm sure he will listen to his body, and if ever need be, get checked. Any sign of blood is an indication, but it is often ruled out as something uncomplicated, like hemorrhoids.

I dedicate this book to Casey, my only birth child and the gift of my life. I used to write him notes throughout his life, starting when I was seven months pregnant. So it is fitting that a book of continued life is left in his possession.

Kent thinks we are meant to be together. He wrote me every day for a year and swears he thought about me every day for 32 years. We hadn't seen each other since 1978. A regret I live with is to have lost touch. My love letters today compare to our teen years. When I shared my emails with my best friend, Mary, she concurred that no woman could resist the love mail I was receiving.

And she was right. I could not resist.

With Zoey (and Piper)

Coloring is Healing

After being diagnosed with stage four colorectal cancer I found coloring to be therapeutic, so I began to color... and color... my Cancer journey.

I would draw images of the radiation machines zapping out the bad cells. Images I colored while my hair fell out by the handfuls. All the pain and fear I colored, and felt an inner healing. I shared all my favorites on Facebook, where I have the most amazing loving support of friends and family. They were always encouraging me to keep on going and coloring. I was thrilled to see many of my friends pick up this wonderful hobby. My mother and I purchased nearly every coloring book we could get our hands on.

February 10, 2015

The tumor did shrink from 6.5 x 8.2 cm to 6.1 x 7.4. My doctor wants me to do two more months of chemo and another major surgery as she called it. Mom and I went out in the hallway and just cried. We just wanted it to be gone. I am finally feeling better, and it's hard to think of starting over. It has taken 5 months to start to feel better and walk well again. I should be focusing on the positive that the cancer hasn't spread, and I am grateful for that. Thank you to everyone for all your support and prayers. My journey isn't over yet but I have so much love coming in and that helps and gives me more courage. ♥

Casey

These are Some Quotes I Like...

I am healthy, wealthy and wise.

What you focus on expands, so focus on feeling good.

Visualize yourself healthy, happy and whole.

Be grateful for your health. When you are grateful for everything you already have, you will soon have more to be grateful for.

While doing things you love, like coloring, you are moving body, mind and soul in the direction of wellness.

I am disease-free and I am a picture of health.

Visualize the illness disappearing and see yourself as healed.

Believe in your treatment. It is there to help you. On the hard days, know that this too shall pass.

Life is a miraculous gift.

The best is yet to come.

Get your hopes up.

Time heals all wounds.

Laughter is the best medicine.

Teach only love, for that is all we are.

Words of Wellness

Appreciate life always.

Good foods.

Exercise.

Sunshine.

Loving friends and family.

Read empowering books.

Use positive affirmations.

Love with all your heart.

Live each day to the fullest.

And always keep your thoughts wishful.

More Favorite Quotes and Words

I want to inspire others by my healing, and in the future I choose to inspire others through all the amazing and pleasant things that effortlessly occur in my life. You are not meant to bear that which you find unpleasant; you are meant to change it.

I don't have bad hair days because I can wear hats and scarves because I have Cancer.

It's not my Cancer because I'm not keeping it.

This reflection is not my true self, because I have Cancer.

I don't mean to offend by the light-hearted look at Cancer. But, it puts most of us in such a dark place that we need the light wherever we can find it.

A book is a dream you hold in your hand.

Books are uniquely potable magic.

Do not anticipate trouble or worry about what may happen. Keep always in the sunlight.
Play, rest, be joyful and expect to be well.

A strong positive attitude will create more miracles than any wonder drug.

Cheerfulness is the principle ingredient in the composition of health.

Affirm: All is well in my world. I am powerful and limitless.

Laughing produces healing chemicals in your body. Find what cracks you up.

Your body knows and functions better when you are happy.

The goal is to have peace of mind.

Refuse to let the infection be your identity. Speak not of it. Don't let it fill your every waking moment. Know it is being healed.

Cancers, as well as other foreign proteins, "come and go" through a lifetime. Our immune system is designed to deal with that and will happily do so if allowed.

Forgive those who missed an earlier diagnosis.

Things I Would Miss the Most

My husband's sweet talk and tenderness.

Chinese food.

My mother's laugh.

Dark chocolate almond popsicles.

Listening to the remarkable way that Casey speaks his language.

Fixing up the house.

Cuddles from Zoey and her making me laugh with her funny ways.

Being proud of my dad and knowing what a good father he was.

The Beach!

My mother's ability to multi-task and her compassionate nature (although I wish she would slow down!)

Springtime

The Happiness Project

Be patient.
Let it go.
Act the way you want to feel.
Be polite and be fair.
Enjoy the process.
No calculation.
There is only love.

Some days you totally fight for the other's sake.

Today I believe I can win. Today I choose to fight. But I reserve the right to quit tomorrow without feeling guilty or like I have let anyone down.

With friends Amy George, Mary Aldridge Devaney,
and Roxanne Manning in 2013

Your Attention, Please

I need your attention and your imagination here for a moment, because I love you. Going to this dark place may save your life.

First, imagine that you have to drink this horrible nasty gallon of a flavored drink. Eat nothing overnight. Imagine spending a couple thousand dollars on this colonoscopy test that you keep hearing you should have. But in your mind, you think you don't need it, think you can't afford it, and think you will have it done some day when you're older.

Imagine going into the clinic for that test and being given a happy pill that makes the room turn a pretty blue and you love the nurses that are blurring in and out of your vision. Imagine waking up and hearing, "All done. See you in ten years."

That is imagination, part one. Now, let's go to another possibility.

Imagine having unexplainable pains... tests... diet changes... antibiotics... pain... Cancer... surgery... colonoscopy... hospital... chemo... radiation... chemo... pain... fights with insurance companies for tests and medications.

Imagine not being able to get out of bed without your morphine pill, Doc saying *Enough*, biopsy, blood work, port, side effects, surgery possibilities, fear of being intimate with your husband again because of bladder, vaginal, rectal issues, reading horrific stories, new friends dying, nurses as best friends, new friends surviving and giving you hope, a suicide pill. Living in fear of it coming back, and scans for the rest of your life, however long.

March 14, 2016

About a year and a half ago I got my port put in to help me through chemo and surgeries. Today is bitter sweet because we are getting ready to go to the hospital this morning to have it removed. I thought this would be the happiest day of my life, meaning the cancer was gone. Sometimes things don't work out as planned but I will still be happy to have it gone. One less thing that has to be taken care of or cause me pain.

March 15, 2016

I appreciate when my doctors, surgeons, nurses, and dentists are kind people. At first I thought I may not like the new dentist much when he asked how long I was expected to live so he could decide which of my teeth to save but then I realized he was just trying to save me some money. Chemo did bad things to my teeth and today I started dental work that hurt worse than the port being removed. Now I feel kinda beat up. Thinking of taking a few days off from doing anything. Needing a break from trying to be courageous, not let people take things out of me for a while. No matter, it is always best to be kind. You never know how hard someone is trying to hold on to some courage.

April 21, 2016

It's benign! Finally some good news, faith, hope, and love to share. The biopsy for the lump that was removed isn't caused from the cancer the way the surgeon thought. I love hearing that. After getting it cut off it has become infected and is very painful and making it impossible for me to sit. A couple of other little infections and a problem with my ostomy and maybe I could start to feel better again. I think I only had two weeks of that after surgery and went all the way back to bed ridden. No matter, I am grateful to hear those words "benign."

April 27, 2016

My doctor told me last week I would die of colorectal cancer, and my first thought was, *How do you know I won't get hit by a car?* That did not need to be put in my head. Talking with a friend has been hard too, because I don't want to talk about being sick. I do that enough with the family. I'm not in denial, just know it's not good for me. She actually mentioned that my two years should just about be up. I don't know how to deal with this. I am really sick. The infections have gotten worse and I can barely walk. But I want people to see me as well even with cancer. My doctor also said she feared this was the cancer coming through, but it makes no sense that my quality of life surgery was just for that short two weeks when I felt better. I couldn't have been gutted just for that. A lot of my problems are from the surgeries and the treatments. But I still feel gratitude for every day.

May 9, 2016

How do you say goodbye?

May 10, 2016

I apologize for not finishing my post yesterday. When I went to see my surgeon, he wanted to hospitalize me to get my vitals up and he confirmed the lump growing out of me is the cancer spreading. Apparently benign can just be scar tissue so those tests seem irrelevant, but he insisted on doing more. I haven't written much to anyone because my hands give out. I just want to sleep, and have lost my appetite again with nausea, so it doesn't look like it will be long... but as accepting as we are trying to be, we aren't giving up hope. Hospice is coming over Friday to help get some pain control figured out. Thank you for your well wishes.

May 16, 2016

My mom is writing this for me because I am unable to do it.

It's time for me to say Goodbye.

Hospice brought me a bed and set it up by my window so I can see outside, the birds, flowers and listen to the raindrops. The nurse will come as often as I like to help me with this transition. Saying goodbye to my family is very hard: my mom, my son Casey, my husband Kent, and my dad, Ralph. My dad came all the way from Republic, Washington to see me today and to say our goodbyes. Chris, my cousin, drove up and brought my dad to me. Thanks to my family, they made this happen. My dog Zoey has not left my side. Thank you for all the love, inspiration and support you have given me through my illness, I love you all. You have kept me alive longer than they said.

Thank you, Mary, for coming over to see me. I would love to see each and every one of you, but it tires me out too much, so I will say my goodbyes to all of you now. Love and hugs. My Mom will post as she can for me. Here is a picture of me and my dad.

Epilogue

On May 20th, 2016, at 11:43, my daughter passed away. Kent and I were both with her to the end, holding her hands. Because she passed away before she could finish her book, I need to bring closure to it for her.

After Tricia's last surgery, she only had about two weeks of good health, and then the pain returned. She was unable to sit normally or comfortably, and could only sit on her side because the pain was so unbearable. She ate very little as the Cancer took over her body, and she was getting very, very sick.

Another tumor grew outside of Tricia's body, and made it impossible for her to sit, stand or lie comfortably. We took her to see her surgeon and were told it was the Cancer, and that removing the newest tumor would only make things worse. We ended up calling Hospice for help in taking care of my child. Kent and I spent every second together with Tricia or taking turns to keep her as comfortable as was possible. We told her we loved her often.

As she lay in her hospital bed, in her own home, she conveyed her love for all of her friends on Facebook. Then she told us: no more food, drink or medication for her pain. She would lift her hand and push the pain medicine away. I made some popsicles with her almond milk and dark chocolate, and she loved them. She also loved ice chips. Kent and I watched her slip away with every shallow breath; we watched her lose her battle with Cancer.

But this story is not over. This story will never end, because all of Tricia's friends have seen and experienced her positive attitude, and they've been inspired in so many ways. And I know they will pass all of this on. Tricia lives in her words and all the love she showed and shared. She touched so many people.

We thank you for letting her into your hearts. We miss her.
~ Rose Graham Miano

What is My Courage
When Compared to You?

for Tricia

I have none,
so much pain
so much loss
so much courage
I admire you
  my niece
  my sister.
Never could I
  find so much hope
  so much love,
  so much strength.
You are in my thoughts,
  my dreams.
Your strength
  will always be embedded
  in me.
Thank you.

~ Sheila Feldmeier

www.ingramcontent.com/pod-product-compliance
Lightning Source LLC
LaVergne TN
LVHW021620080426
835510LV00019B/2685